DATE DUE

MAR 17 2016			
MAR 0			

Coping with

AGGRESSION

Patricia Emanuele

The Rosen Publishing Group, Inc.
New York

Published in 2001 by The Rosen Publishing Group, Inc.
29 East 21st Street, New York, NY 10010

First Edition

Cover photo © Benelux Press/IndexStock

Library of Congress Cataloging-in-Publication Data

Emanuele, Patricia
Coping with aggression / Patricia Emanuele.
p. cm. — (Coping)
Includes bibliographical references and index.
Summary: Explores social and scientific theories about the causes of aggression and suggests several strategies for coping with aggression.
ISBN 0-8239-3360-1 (lib.)
1. Aggressiveness in adolescence—Juvenile literature
[1. Aggressiveness 2. Anger 3. Violence]
I. Title II. Series
BF724.3.A34 E63 2001
                                                      2001-002763

155.5—dc21

Manufactured in the United States of America

Contents

Introduction

The word "aggression" has many meanings and applies to many circumstances. In the military, it refers to a hostile invasion. In medicine, it can refer to a rapidly progressive disease. People also use the term "aggressive drivers" to refer to drivers who yell, swear, and cut wildly in and out of traffic. Aggressive driving causes serious accidents and, in some cases, death. In sports, aggression can refer to the drive and determination used to achieve a goal. A soccer player practices, builds up strength, plans moves, and aggressively goes for the ball and scores a goal. A political candidate might win an election as a result of an aggressive campaign by making speeches, sending out flyers, and getting votes.

In recent years, the media has placed a lot of emphasis on the subject of teenagers and aggression. Consider the following examples of tragic events—examples of aggressive adolescent behavior—that have shocked the public.

Santee, California
On March 5, 2001, a fifteen-year-old high school student opens fire, killing two students and wounding thirteen others.

Littleton, Colorado
On April 20, 1999, two high school students on a shooting spree kill twelve students, one teacher, and themselves.

Springfield, Oregon
On May 21, 1998, two teens are killed and twenty people are hurt when a fifteen-year-old student opens fire in the high school cafeteria. His parents are later found dead.

Fayetteville, Tennessee
On May 19, 1998, an eighteen-year-old honor student kills a classmate who was dating his ex-girlfriend.

Edinboro, Pennsylvania
On April 24, 1998, a teacher is shot by a fourteen-year-old in front of students at an eighth-grade dance.

Jonesboro, Arkansas
On March 24, 1998, four girls and a teacher are shot by two boys at a middle school.

West Paducah, Kentucky
On December 1, 1997, three students are killed and five wounded by a fourteen-year-old student.

Pearl, Mississippi
On October 1, 1997, a sixteen-year-old boy kills his mother and then goes to school and shoots nine students, killing two.

In an attempt to respond to the public's horror at these events, a number of professional organizations have been studying adolescent anger, how aggression develops, and how to prevent or cope with it. Some researchers have found out that aggression plays a part in vandalism, burglary, cruelty, substance abuse, and gang violence. And, unfortunately, many young people not only exhibit these behaviors but also leave victims in their wakes.

Aggression plays a major role in the lives of adolescents. Even teens who may not be involved in situations that are characterized by aggression are aware of this sort of behavior. In a recent American Psychological Association poll, 40 percent of youth say that they have concerns about a potentially violent classmate. The survey also revealed that nearly three out of four youths want to know more about how to recognize the warning signs of violent behavior.

According to the American Academy of Child and Adolescent Psychiatry's (AACAP) 1999 Violence Fact Sheet, teens experience and exhibit aggressive behaviors in a number of ways.

AACAP 1999 Violence Fact Sheet

➪ In 1996, the National Center on Child Abuse and Neglect reported 969,018 cases of violent crimes committed against children.

➪ In 1996 and 1997, 10 percent of all public schools reported at least one serious violent crime to police or law enforcement (Bureau of Justice Statistics and Office of Juvenile Justice and Delinquency Prevention, U.S. Department of Justice).

➤ Gunshot wounds to children ages sixteen and under have increased 300 percent in major urban areas since 1986.

➤ According to Federal Bureau of Investigation (FBI) reports, 2,900 juveniles were arrested for murder in 1996.

➤ Estimates indicate that as many as 5,000 children die each year as a result of mistreatment and abuse from parents or guardians.

➤ Every day in America, sixteen children and youths are killed by firearms, according to a Children's Defense Fund study in 1998.

➤ Nearly a million U.S. students took guns to school during 1998 (Parents Resource Institute for Drug Education).

➤ Each year, 123,400 children are arrested for violent crimes in the United States (Office of Juvenile Justice and Delinquency Prevention, 1997).

➤ Persons under the age of twenty-five account for approximately 50 percent of all victims of a serious violent crime (Institute for Youth Development, 1998).

Aggression Is a Behavior

Aggression is a verbal or physical action that is usually undertaken with the intent to injure. Verbal aggression can include being overly critical, name-calling, accusing someone of having immoral or despicable traits or motives, spreading rumors, nagging, whining, being sarcastic, or exhibiting prejudice. Physical aggression—which can escalate to deadly violence—consists of hitting, biting, kicking, or throwing objects.

Is it bad to feel angry? No. Anger is beneficial when it motivates us to change a bad situation. We can learn how to manage our anger. But there is no justification for physical harm, violent aggression, or psychological insult to another person.

Aggression is not an emotion per se, but it is frequently associated with anger. However, anger and aggression are not synonymous. Anger is an emotion, and aggression is a behavior. It is normal to feel angry, but how we experience and express our anger depends on many factors. Anger may feel painful or explosive. We may feel angry with others or with ourselves. Things that make some people angry will not necessarily bother other people. Sometimes we do not even know why we are angry. Most important, it is very possible to be angry without causing harm. Though there are times when aggression can be positive (to be discussed later), more often than not, aggression causes harm—be it to ourselves, to others, or both.

Aggression can be positive when it plays a role in helping us reach a goal, without the intent to harm or exact revenge. This positive aggression can help athletes train and compete more aggressively or energize anyone who is hoping to attain a desired goal. This form of aggression can be intense, but it is positively focused and task-oriented.

However, our focus here is learning how to cope with aggression that is detrimental, such as the kind illustrated in the following scenario.

Jeff and Roy

Jeff, fifteen, was the third child of Sally and Randolf Holmes. Their eldest child, Nancy, lived away at college, and Roy, seventeen, was the athlete in the family. Roy was always a good student and a respectful son. He was recruited by several colleges and offered numerous scholarships.

Jeff had never been a motivated or bright student. He was not interested in sports, and he had always felt like a failure compared to his brother. Jeff and Roy often argued. For years, Roy had secretly mistreated Jeff. When the boys were younger, their parents dismissed Roy's aggressive behavior toward his brother as "roughhousing." But Roy often left Jeff bruised, and Roy threatened to hurt his brother if he complained to their parents. At one point, Roy even threw lit cigarettes at Jeff while he sat petrified with fear on the living room couch.

Jeff spent most of his time at home in his room listening to music. Consequently, his grades got progressively worse. His lack of communication at home was starting to create stress for his family. It seemed as though he would get angry at the smallest criticisms his parents made. He would often refuse to get out of bed. Though he used to fear the thought of missing a class, now he would cut the whole day and hide out at the park.

Jeff's parents tried talking to him, but Jeff would glare at them stony-eyed. They even took him to various doctors who suggested counseling.

The purpose of this book is to discuss factors that influence aggression like Roy's. We will also cover coping strategies that will aid you in dealing with either your own aggression or that of people around you. Learning about anger and aggression is a first step in addressing these concerns because understanding often helps increase your ability to cope.

Anger and Aggression

"He pushed me, so I hit him," said Lisa.

"She got on my nerves, so I smacked her," said Max.

"He was moving too slowly, so I kicked him," said Sing.

Anger

Anger—like guilt, excitement, or sadness—is an emotion, a feeling. There are two basic types of anger: One is healthy, and the other is unhealthy and destructive. Healthy anger is a legitimate response to injustice, abuse, and loss. Destructive anger often stems from feelings of inadequacy and/or frustration. In other words, people demonstrate destructive anger in order to dominate and control. Frequently, this is a subconscious desire.

Anger can be expressed in many forms, such as cynicism, pouting, and physical violence. Anger can also be denied. However, unexpressed anger can lead to hostility and being overly critical. Some people are easily angered and are less tolerant of frustrations, inconveniences, and annoyances. One reason for this may be genetics. Individuals may inherit a trait to anger easily or feel impatient and frustrated to the point of violence. Another reason may be socio-cultural. In *Anger: The Misunderstood Emotion* (1982), Carol Tavris writes about how our emotions are subject to the laws of learning just like other behaviors. Perhaps aggressive behavior (or the ability to control it) is teachable, rather than an inherited trait.

What Triggers Anger?

Managing anger is dependent on taking responsibility for your emotions. One of the first and most positive steps in dealing with potentially destructive anger that might lead to aggressive behavior is to find out what triggers the anger in question.

If you are the angry person, you should be aware that your anger can affect your academic performance, can lead to feelings of isolation, and can affect your relationships with family, teachers, and friends. Anger usually erupts in response to the following four triggers:

1. Mistreatment: unkind words, ridicule, name-calling, and/or physical abuse

2. Unfairness: being falsely accused of something

9

3. Disappointment: when your expectations are not met

4. Nuisances: irritants and annoyances, such as loud noises, long lines, or traffic

Forms of Aggression

Negative aggression can manifest itself either verbally or physically.

Verbal Aggression

- ⇌ Criticizing

- ⇌ Finding fault in everyone

- ⇌ Name-calling

- ⇌ Excessive yelling or screaming

- ⇌ Accusing someone of immoral or despicable traits

- ⇌ Excessive nagging

- ⇌ Excessive use of sarcasm

- ⇌ Prejudice

- ⇌ Spreading rumors

Physical Aggression

- ⇌ Slapping

↩ Shoving

↩ Kicking

↩ Hitting

↩ Pushing

↩ Using weapons

Outward Aggression

Some psychologists have categorized aggression that is directed outward, or toward others, into two types: reactive aggression and proactive aggression. Reactive aggression is also called impulsive aggression, and some people refer to proactive aggression as instrumental aggression.

Reactive aggression is an automatic response to an immediate threat. It is intended to hurt by means of threatening or invoking fear in another person. It is marked by strong emotions, especially anger. For example, a person who has been mugged wants to fight back and hurt his or her assailant.

Proactive aggression is cold-blooded and seemingly emotionless. It is aggressive behavior exhibited as a means to a specific end—for example, a criminal who mugs someone with the intent of stealing money. This type of aggressor treats people as objects, and the aggression can continue despite any ensuing punishment.

Passive Aggression

Another form of aggression is expressed by being passive and oppositional. This is called passive-aggression.

A person exhibiting passive-aggressive behavior might become argumentative, exaggerate others' faults, procrastinate, pretend to agree, become tearful, or deny that he or she is angry.

Bullying

Bullying is another form of aggression. Bullying, in the form of teasing, taunting, threatening, hitting, and stealing, may be initiated by one or more people against a victim. The victim is deliberately excluded and is socially isolated.

Those who engage in bullying need to feel powerful and in control. They derive satisfaction from inflicting suffering and seem to have no empathy for their victims. Chronic adolescent bullies seem to carry their aggressive behaviors into adulthood, thus negatively influencing their ability to develop and maintain positive relationships.

Inward Aggression

Aggression can also be directed inward, which can ultimately lead to self-destructive behavior and even suicide. Often, teens who are depressed become irritable and aggressive rather than despondent. K. M. Thompson, et al., in the article "The Neglected Link Between Eating Disturbances and Aggressive Behavior in Girls," published in the *Journal of the American Academy of Child and Adolescent Psychiatry* (October 1999), notes an association between eating disorders and aggression in young women. This suggests that anger may be directed inward and be expressed by self-destructive behavior. Thus, it is not surprising that many teenage girls develop eating disorders such as anorexia nervosa and bulimia. It is possible that these young women are angry, and by turning their anger inward, they use food as a means of expressing or reacting to their emotions.

Gender Differences

Men and women tend to express aggression differently. This is due in part to socialization, or the training children receive as to what is expected and appropriate behavior for boys and girls. Parents of young boys may say "boys will be boys" in response to hitting, kicking, or pushing. Parents of young girls may simply say "be good." We may still be surprised when we hear of women getting into physical fights, whereas the idea of men fighting does not often strike us as being unusual.

According to statistics reported in the *1999 Annual Report on School Safety,* published by the Departments of Education and Justice, the overall rate for violent crime has declined. Nevertheless, crime remains a problem concentrated within certain geographic locations. Men in all ethnic and racial groups remain more likely to commit violent acts of aggression and be victims of such acts than women. Therefore, most research on aggression has focused on males.

Although teenage males commit more violent acts, teenage females' involvement in delinquency and crime has increased in the last two decades. Like male aggression, aggression expressed by female adolescents is often associated with disputes over a significant other, a need to uphold a reputation, expressions of rage toward a disliked person, and reactions to real or imagined gossip.

Females are more apt to spread rumors, exclude someone from a group, engage in psychological bullying, or exhibit passive-aggressive behavior. This type of aggression can be as painful as physical aggression, and it can even escalate into physical attacks.

Aggressive people may themselves have been victims of neglect, abuse, poverty, and/or violence. Increased exposure to violence in the media, and less overall respect and trust of traditional and established authority figures may also contribute to the increase in aggression exhibited by women and girls.

Interestingly, reports also reveal that physical aggression may increase a girl's feelings of empowerment, dominance, and self-importance. Teenage girls who act aggressively say that they get attention and respect from their peers and feel that it is worth the disciplinary measures they encounter precisely because they feel powerful. Hopefully, more future studies will explore the relationship between social, personal, and societal power and aggressive behavior in women and girls.

What Causes Aggression?

There are many competing theories regarding the causes of aggression in children and teens. Some blame the glorification of violence in our culture, easy access to guns, growing up in an economically disadvantaged and violent neighborhood, and many hours of inadequate supervision. Despite the fact that a problem seems to have emerged, our society tends to overlook aggression, especially in the form of physical violence, until dramatic incidents such as school shootings occur.

Biological Causes

Many prominent scientific theorists and researchers have argued that human beings are genetically predisposed for aggression, that people are born with aggressive instincts. Sigmund Freud (1856–1939) was an Austrian psychiatrist and commonly considered to be the founder of psychoanalysis. He believed that all humans possess an unconscious aggressive drive from birth.

Another Austrian scientist, Konrad Lorenz (1903–1989), argued that people and animals depend upon an aggressive instinct for survival. This natural instinct to protect and defend one's territory and offspring ensures that only the strongest survive. In the late 1930s, American psychologist John Dollard (1900–1980) believed that any sort of frustration resulted in an aggressive response.

In the early twentieth century, two American scientists, Nettie Maria Stevens and Edmund Beccher Hilson, independently offered evidence that, of the forty-six human chromosomes (proteins that contain genes), females always carry one pair of two matching X chromosomes (XX), while males have only one X paired with one Y (XY). In the 1970s, it was suggested that men who were born with an extra chromosome were more likely to display episodes of aggressive behavior than men who were not born with this extra chromosome. About three out of one thousand men inherit an extra X or Y chromosome—meaning that a male would be XYY or XXY instead of XY. However, at present, this theory remains inconclusive.

Brain Disturbances

The adult brain weighs about three pounds and is the size of a grapefruit. It is full of billions of microscopic cells called neurons that send messages throughout the brain and body with the help of chemical substances called neurotransmitters. Sometimes, an imbalance in one of the over forty neurotransmitters in the brain can cause an emotional or behavioral disorder. These disorders can manifest themselves in aggressive behavior.

Any damage to the brain resulting from brain tumors, stroke, or head injuries may foster aggressive behavior. Motor vehicle crashes, recreational injuries, violent assaults, and head trauma during birth can also damage areas of the brain. This in turn can have an adverse effect on emotions, behavior, and intelligence. Several studies have shown that brain dysfunction can be seen in images such as PET (positron emission tomography) scans of the brain and electroencephalograms, which measure brain waves.

The brain has three major sections: the cerebrum, the cerebellum, and the brain stem. The cerebrum fills the main part of the skull. The cerebellum is at the back base of the head and is important for movement, posture, and coordination. The brain stem connects the brain to the spinal cord and regulates breathing, the heartbeat, blood pressure, digestion, and swallowing. The cerebrum is the largest area of the brain. It has two layers: the cerebral cortex and the limbic system. The outer layer is the cerebral cortex. The inner layer is called the limbic system.

The brain is also divided into four sections or lobes: frontal, parietal, temporal, and occipital lobes. Each lobe is responsible for overseeing different functions. The frontal lobe is located around the forehead. Part of the frontal lobe along with the cortex is called the prefrontal cortex. It is thought to be important in restraining impulsive outbursts, even those associated with aggression.

A thin sheet called the cerebral cortex encases the brain. No one fully understands how the brain works, but scientists and researchers think that the cortex is the decision-making part of the brain. The interior portion of the brain is responsible for emotions and is known as the limbic system.

The limbic system lies deep within the brain. Scientists have found other areas of the brain involved in the experience of and expression of aggression. These include the amygdala, hippocampus, and hypothalamus. The amygdala are small almond-shaped structures located in the internal portion of the brain near the temporal lobes. They are thought to act as an emotional center and may be key to understanding and controlling aggression. Nearby is the crescent-shaped structure called the hippocampus. It is believed to be important in storing memories. The hypothalamus is part of the limbic system and is located in the internal portion of the brain near the base. It is responsible for emotions.

Low Levels of a Brain Chemical

It is suggested that a low level of the brain chemical serotonin can result in increased aggressive behavior. Serotonin is a neurotransmitter that helps send messages between brain cells. It is believed to function as a behavior inhibitor. Low levels of serotonin can contribute to uncontrolled behavior. However, not all individuals with low levels of serotonin are violent.

Diet and Nutrition

Specific foods have been linked to aggressive behavior. Carol Tavris describes how some foods—eggs, chocolate, milk, cola, corn, and bacon—have been known to produce mood changes ranging from mild to depression or even hyperactivity. According to Tavris, some people are sensitive to the chemical additives in food. Eliminating certain foods from your diet might help reduce the intensity of some symptoms.

In addition, a diet that is high in refined carbohydrates such as sweets and processed foods can affect blood glucose levels and influence aggressive behavior. A 1997 article written by Amos Shoenthaler in the *Journal of Nutritional and Environmental Medicine* cited two studies. One was a 1982 study of juvenile offenders ages twelve to eighteen that related a drop in disciplinary offenses to a reduction in the consumption of refined carbohydrates.

Another study monitored sixty-two confined male and female delinquents, ranging in age from thirteen to seventeen. They were studied for three months. In the experiment, the youths were randomly assigned to two groups. One group received vitamin and mineral supplements, and the other received placebos, fake vitamins (or medicines). The supplements contained twelve vitamins and eleven minerals. The eating habits of those being studied were recorded. Blood concentrations of nutrients were monitored before and after the experiment. The results demonstrated better behavior and less violence when previously low blood concentrations of vitamins and minerals were increased. It is suggested that lowering fats and sugars and eating more fruits, vegetables, and whole grains may contribute to a reduction in aggressive impulses.

Narcissism

In the past, it was thought that low self-esteem resulted in aggression. However, more recent research and studies indicate that this may not be true. Psychologists Brad Bushman and Roy Baumeister in their article

"Threatened Egotism, Narcissism, Self-Esteem, and Direct and Displaced Aggression: Does Self-Love or Self-Hate Lead to Violence?" published in the July 1998 edition of the *Journal of Personality and Social Psychology* argued that narcissism may in fact be the real problem. Narcissists are people who have an unrealistic, overinflated, and superior opinion of themselves. Anyone who threatens a narcissist's favorable view of himself or herself can become a target of that person's aggression.

Behavioral Disorders

Aggression can also be a symptom of various behavioral disorders, including attention deficit hyperactivity disorder (ADHD), conduct disorder, and oppositional defiant disorder. The American Psychiatric Association publishes a book called *The Diagnostic and Statistical Manual of Mental Disorders (DSM-IV)*, now in its fourth edition, which provides extensive details on the symptoms of every mental disorder. However, if you think that you may have a behavioral disorder, or that someone close to you has one, do not try to diagnose it yourself. While the DSM-IV is a good resource, any diagnosis needs to be conducted by a mental health professional.

An accurate diagnosis and treatment regime may consist of medications, individual and/or family therapy, or behavioral modifications. As therapists and psychiatrists frequently diagnose teenagers as suffering from depression and behavior disorders, aggressive behavior is often considered a symptom rather than a disorder itself.

Depression

It is normal to feel sad from time to time. But when your feelings and behavior are preventing you from functioning properly on a daily basis, professional help may be necessary. If you are experiencing severe or clinical depression, finding the proper treatment is possible. Some signs of depression may include:

- Sudden and sustained irritability or moodiness

- A lack of interest in formerly pleasurable activities

- Fatigue or lethargy

- Difficulty concentrating

- Changes in sleep patterns

- Changes in appetite

- Feelings of guilt, hopelessness, and/or helplessness

- Abuse of drugs or other self-destructive behaviors

- Suicidal thoughts

- Excessive crying and/or sadness

More Than Just Anger: Jermaine's Tale

Jermaine, sixteen, hated her life. Her mom sent her to live with her dad after she had tried to hurt her baby half-sister. It was the last straw—Jermaine had continuously tried to make trouble between her mom and her mom's new husband.

New home, new school, new teachers . . . Jermaine had too much to handle. She did not want to do any work, did not want to make friends, did not eat, and could not sleep. One day, when she was bored, Jermaine was in the school bathroom, tearing her history notes from her binder and flushing them down the toilet. What did she care about dumb old history?

While Jermaine was destroying her notes, a custodian came into the bathroom to clean up. Jermaine came out of the bathroom stall, took one look at the custodian, and couldn't stop thinking about how pathetic the custodian was. The custodian just spent her days cleaning up after people who didn't care about the world anymore. People like Jermaine.

The next thing Jermaine knew, she was yelling at the custodian and pushing her out the door. Later that day, Jermaine was sent to see the principal and the school counselor.

"How can we make you want to be here and learn?" Laurie, the counselor, asked.

"Just kill me," Jermaine replied.

Jermaine's parents were called right away. Professional help was sought, and Jermaine was hospitalized for about a month. She received psychotherapy, medication, and tutoring. Long-term family therapy is planned.

A Learned
Behavior?

We have defined aggression as a behavior and discussed some possible causes and factors that might contribute to the exhibition of aggressive behavior. But is aggression toward others a learned behavior? According to social learning theory—which argues that attitudes and behaviors are learned from our families, friends, and environment—it is.

Social Learning Theory

Until the mid-twentieth century, many people within the scientific community believed that humans were innately aggressive and that inborn drives and motivations caused aggressive behavior. As researchers further studied human behavior, some found that many factors, both environmental and genetic, influenced how a person acts. This marked the development of social learning theory.

Social learning theorists propose that when children watch others, they learn many forms of behavior, ranging from sharing and cooperation to aggression. One of the leading advocates of social learning theory is psychologist and researcher Albert Bandura. Born in 1925 in Canada, he now resides in the United States. Bandura observed that if an action is positively reinforced, it is likely to be repeated.

Contrastingly, if actions are punished, they are less likely to be repeated. In *Social Foundations of Thought and Action: A Social Cognitive Theory* (1986), he states that children who see aggressive behavior punished are less likely to exhibit aggression. In contrast, when positive behaviors are rewarded, positive behaviors are imitated. Social learning theorists contend that when children and teenagers exhibit aggressive behaviors, they are mimicking behaviors they have already witnessed.

The Family

The family plays a major role in the development, maintenance, and/or decline of aggression. Parents are often the most influential role models for their children. Children who observe violent parents are likely to be influenced by that behavior. The family is typically the primary mechanism for setting limits as well as for providing support, encouragement, and safety. When a young child yells, shoves, or hits as a means of getting what he or she wants, and he or she gets away with this sort of behavior, the child learns to repeat that behavior.

Abuse

Children who have been hit by their parents sometimes grow up to hit their own children and to abuse their partners. Several studies have linked early physical and sexual abuse in children to the exhibition of aggressive behaviors later on. In a study in the May 2000 *Journal of Marriage and Family Counseling,* researchers S. Swinford, A. DeMaris, S. Cernkovich, and P. Giordano suggested that harsh physical punishment in childhood is directly related to violence against a partner later in life. In the article that reported their findings, "Harsh Physical Discipline in Childhood and Violence in Later Romantic Involvements: The Mediating Role of Problem Behaviors," they suggest that harsh physical punishment of children by their parents or guardians enhances the likelihood that the child will exhibit problem behaviors later in life. A child who is the victim of sexual abuse may also have difficulty relating to others especially as he or she reaches adulthood, according to a 1998 report published by the American Academy of Child and Adolescent Psychiatry.

It is important to note that abuse can be verbal as well as physical. Verbal aggression can be very damaging. Being part of a household where a child constantly hears statements such as "You're stupid," "You always do it wrong," or "No one likes you" is very detrimental.

Discipline

Children who are disciplined harshly may be more likely to engage in deviant behavior. These behaviors may include problem drinking, substance abuse, and physical violence toward themselves or others. Lax discipline practices may also result in aggressive behavior later in life. If a child's primary caregiver does not set appropriate limits for the child, he or she may grow up lacking an understanding of self-control and emotional boundaries.

Other Factors

There are other family dynamics and factors that might contribute to the onset of aggressive behavior.

➤ Families characterized by discord.

➤ Lack of affection.

➤ Families in which there is a lot of parent-to-parent conflict and aggression. (In *Lost Boys: Why Our Sons Turn Violent and How We Can Save Them*, psychologist James Garbarino writes that parents of aggressive children are often very aggressive themselves. Adolescents who have been exposed to family aggression are more likely to use aggression toward peers and during dating, marriage, and child rearing.

➤ Poor supervision.

➤ Families in which a parent has been imprisoned. The Justice Department's Bureau of Justice Statistics reports nearly 1.5 million American children have a mother or father in federal or state prison. The social disadvantages of being the child of a parent who is incarcerated can result in a lack of discipline, neglect, and economic hardship.

↪ Families in which substance abuse is a problem. When a child grows up in this situation, his or her aggression is most likely due to anger—anger at the parent who is the substance abuser or anger at the nonabusing parent for not taking any action to change the situation. These children may not even know why they are angry, but they are often aggressive.

It can be a challenge to identify which specific family factors contribute to the development of aggression. While many adolescents may face similar problems, a minority of them commit aggressive acts. Many are resilient and cope. They become well-adjusted, responsible, and productive adults and members of society.

Beyond the Family

Attitudes and behaviors are also learned through relationships and associations outside of the immediate family. Many factors influencing aggression may relate to nonfamily factors. It is also important to remember that there are a combination of factors leading to aggression, and very often no one factor can be blamed.

Peer Rejection

As adolescents distance themselves from their parents and begin to become aware of and assert their own identities, they often seek support from their friends. As we discussed earlier, social learning theory explains that during adolescence, attitudes and behaviors are learned through associations. For teenagers, friendships, cliques, and informal social groupings often replace the family and provide positive and useful places to develop and practice social skills.

Peer group acceptance is important. Adolescents need to feel that they belong. This cannot be underestimated; being excluded is painful. Some adolescents feel socially rejected for various reasons that may include the aggressive behavior of others communicated in unkind reactions to their physical appearance or due to racial or religious prejudice. There is a risk that, out of frustration and desperation, these individuals might also become aggressive.

Bullies

Bullying is primarily a group phenomenon that is largely enabled and maintained by group members. Adolescents often turn to their peer groups to observe and learn social behavior and social attitudes. If groups exhibit high rates of aggression, group members may become aggressive.

Students who are victims of bullying miss school days each year because they fear being humiliated, injured, or even killed. Some students who tease their peers do so in an effort to be accepted by bullies but feel uncomfortable with their own behavior.

Interestingly, it seems that people who have been bullied often become bullies themselves. Bullies can be both victims of aggression and perpetrators of aggression. Because bullying is so rampant, this is an issue that requires home, school, and community attention and intervention.

Although many Americans claim that violence among American young people is a major concern, bullying is infrequently addressed and little national data on instances of bullying are available. In a study published in the April 25, 2001, edition of the *Journal of the American Medical Association*, researchers Tonja R. Nansel, Mary Overpeck, Ramani S. Pilla, W. June Ruan, Bruce Simons-Morton, and Peter Scheidt sampled 15,686 students in grades six through ten in public and private schools throughout the United States.

A total of almost 24 percent of the sample reported moderate or frequent involvement in bullying: 13 percent as bullies and nearly 11 percent as those who were bullied. Males were more likely than females to be both perpetrators and targets of bullying. The frequency of bullying was higher among sixth- through eighth-grade students than among ninth- and tenth-grade students. The study concluded that the prevalence of bullying among children and teens in the United States is indeed substantial and that the issue of bullying requires serious attention, both for future research and preventive intervention measures.

Psychologist Dan Ohveus of Sweden describes how schools in Norway addressed bullying in his 1993 book *Bullying at School: What We Know and What We Can Do.* Efforts to reduce bullying in Norwegian schools were undertaken in 1982 after three students committed suicide, in part because they were victims of bullying. Teachers and parents were informed about types of bullying behaviors and why bullying must not be tolerated. Teachers were encouraged to have classroom discussions about bullying and were advised to apply consistent sanctions against bullying. Teachers and parents were encouraged to praise avoidance of bullying. Two years after the campaign, it was found that bullying had declined and students were more satisfied with school.

Portrait of a Bully

Often, people who engage in bullying behavior do so because they need to feel powerful and in control. They seem to have little empathy for their victims. While both males and females can be bullies, some studies have found that females are more apt to use indirect strategies, such as spreading rumors. Regardless, the end result is the same— social isolation for the victim.

Adolescents who are bullied are often anxious, insecure, and cautious, and have low self-esteem. They may lack social skills and friends. A bully's aggressive behavior can have negative effects on a victim's ability to progress both academically and socially.

Media Exposure, the Internet, and Video Games

Exposure to incidents of aggression portrayed in the media, on the Internet, or in video games may contribute to the onset of aggressive behavior in the viewer. That said, studies have yet to prove a direct correlation. Although many adolescents have access to electronic games, the Internet, and images of violence on television, in movies, and in music videos, only a few commit aggressive acts. Nevertheless, exposure to media violence is often associated with involvement in violent aggression, either as a victim or a perpetrator.

Some of the nation's most prestigious medical and mental health groups, such as the American Medical Association, the American Academy of Pediatrics, and the American Academy of Child and Adolescent Psychiatry, have declared that aggression in the media may contribute to increasingly aggressive behavior among people. These groups believe that viewing violence in movies, on television, and in video games, and hearing violent lyrics in music may lead to an increase in aggressive attitudes, values, and behavior. Children who see a lot of violence are more likely to view violence as an effective way of settling conflicts, and they may think that it is acceptable behavior. Further, viewing aggression may lead to emotional desensitization toward aggression in real life.

The American Academy of Child and Adolescent Psychiatry stated in a May 2000 fact sheet that there is concern about the negative and destructive themes of some music, especially music that glorifies violence, abuse of women, and disrespect for authority. This music might pose a danger when adolescents are persistently exposed to seriously destructive messages. This continued exposure may cause changes in behavior or attitudes.

Extensive viewing of television violence may cause greater aggressiveness. On July 27, 2000, at a public health meeting in Washington, DC, the American Medical Association, the American Academy of Pediatrics, the American Psychological Association, and the American Academy of Child and Adolescent Psychiatry all stated that children who see a lot of violence on television are more likely to view violence as an effective way of coping. There is also a link between violent video games and aggression. Psychologist and researcher Craig Anderson reported in the April 2000 *Journal of Personality and Social Psychology* that exposure to violent video games increases aggressive behavior.

The Internet

The Internet provides access to knowledge and information. However, many Web sites promote sexism, violence, and racism. Jane Ellen Stevens's "Online Report 2" on Discover.com's "Hate and Violence: No Simple Answers," reports that there are roughly 400 Web sites preaching hate among approximately 13 million sites. These sites are available to millions of people and may possibly incite aggressive attitudes and behaviors.

We remain unsure of the precise cause (or causes) of aggression. It may stem from biological instinct, one's environment, or a combination of biological and environmental factors. Nevertheless, we do know a great deal about the negative effects of aggressive behavior. Unfortunately, sometimes aggressive actions can lead to harmful and illegal ends.

Unlawful Behavior

David and Kyle are a motley duo who are well-suited to each other; they both feel ignored by their parents, and they are both disliked by their teachers and bullied by their classmates. They are now ready for some Saturday night fun.

Tonight, they have phone numbers in their hands. Cans of spray paint and a baseball bat are left by the front door so that these items will not be forgotten.

"Okay, Kyle, you go first," said David.

Kyle dialed the number. Carol's mother answered.

"Oh, Mrs. Smith," he sighed. "I'm sorry to tell you this, but there has been a terrible accident. Carol was hit by a car, and she's dead."

Kyle slammed down the receiver, and the two laughed hysterically.

"It will serve the little witch right for making fun of me in the lunchroom," grinned Kyle.

It was David's turn next.

33

"Hello, is this the state hospital?" David asked.

"Yes. Where can I direct your call?" asked the operator.

"To anybody who wants to know where a bomb is planted! You have two hours to find the bomb or a whole wing gets blasted!" he exclaimed.

Afterward, the two got in Kyle's car, guzzling beer along the way. The first stop was the parking lot of a local bank. Spray painting graffiti along the outside wall was exciting!

Hopping back into the car, they sped away and cruised through town. They turned off on a remote road. David got the baseball bat. Kyle slowed down the car while David hung out the window to bash mailboxes.

Later that evening, Kyle and David were arrested and taken to a juvenile facility.

Juvenile Delinquency: A High Price to Pay

Aggressive behavior can lead to illegal behavior. In the case of a minor, an individual under the age of eighteen, this behavior is often characterized as juvenile delinquency. Juvenile delinquency is very costly. There is the cost of running the juvenile justice system, the cost of rehabilitation and property damages, and the emotional pain and suffering endured by both the crime victims and the families of the perpetrators.

The Juvenile Justice System

Young people who break the law usually enter the juvenile justice system. Juvenile law varies from state to state and even within states, and it can vary from community to community. There are some fairly general processes, though.

If a juvenile is picked up by law enforcement officers, officials decide whether to send the matter further into the justice system or to divert the case out of the system into an alternative program. Usually this decision is made after consulting the parents and reviewing the juvenile's record of any prior illegal activity. Approximately 30 percent of all juvenile cases were handled within the police department and then released.

Most juvenile court cases stem from law enforcement arrests, but sometimes parents and schools refer juveniles to the courts. Officials known as intake officers review the complaint against the juvenile and the circumstances of the case, and then decide to dismiss the case, handle it informally, or request a formal intervention by the juvenile court. If officials decide to prosecute formally (which usually occurs if previously informal interventions have failed), prosecutors may file a case either in juvenile or criminal court.

Substance Use and Abuse

Experimentation with alcohol and drugs during adolescence is common. Unfortunately, some adolescents quickly progress from first-time use to substance dependency. This is one reason why substance use and abuse is extremely dangerous for adolescents. In a 1997 report on alcohol and drug abuse by the American Academy of Child and Adolescent Psychiatry, half the deaths of people ages fifteen to twenty-four from accidents, homicides, and suicides involve alcohol and/or drug abuse.

The U.S. Centers for Disease Control and Prevention (CDC) surveys teenagers every two years to monitor their risky behaviors. In 1999, 15,349 teens across the United States were surveyed. The CDC survey reported that 26.7 percent of teens smoke marijuana; 4 percent use cocaine; and 50 percent use alcohol. Many of these substances are risk factors linked to aggressive behavior.

Drugs that are readily available to teens include alcohol, prescribed medications, inhalants, and over-the-counter products for things like colds or weight control. In addition, some teenage athletes are at risk for using anabolic steroids. Some athletes try to increase muscle mass by using high doses of anabolic steroids. One result of steroid use is aggressive behavior.

The Right to Bear Arms

According to a 1994 report from the CDC, homicide is the second leading cause of death for youths between the ages of fifteen and twenty-four. The vast majority of these homicides result from firearms. And of course, putting a firearm in the hands of someone who is aggressive is a recipe for disaster.

The 1994 report found that gunfire kills twelve times as many children under age fourteen in the United States as in twenty-five other industrialized nations combined. Although the United States's firearm homicide rate has been declining since 1992, the United States recorded nine times as many handgun homicides per capita as Canada in 1996.

Weapons contribute to unintentional and intentional injuries and deaths. In a 1997 survey, the CDC sampled approximately 1,700 high school students nationwide. It discovered that 18 percent of the students had carried a weapon to school within the preceding thirty days.

Bruises, Not Love

Arlene felt lonely after her best friend, Jessica, began dating Marcus. At first, Jessica would phone Arlene and tell her everything about her dates with Marcus— where they went, what happened, who was there, and all the usual details.

As time went by, Jessica's calls to Arlene became less and less frequent until they finally stopped. Arlene's attempts to call were always met with busy signals, and the messages she left on Jessica's answering machine were not returned.

Arlene missed the fun times she had with Jessica— shopping, doing homework together, listening to music, and just hanging out. Even at school, it seemed as though Jessica had changed. She was quiet and almost timid, and Marcus always seemed to be close by. When talking to Jessica and Marcus, Arlene noticed that Marcus always interrupted Jessica or answered for her. Arlene thought Marcus seemed a little bossy.

One day, the girls were changing into their gym clothes when Arlene noticed bruises on her friend's arms.

"What are those marks from?" Arlene asked.

Jessica hurried to get covered up. "Oh, nothing," she mumbled.

Urging her friend to tell the truth, Arlene demanded, "Please tell me what's going on! We used to be so close and we shared everything. I miss you, and now I'm worried about those bruises on your arms. What's going on?"

Jessica couldn't look her friend in the eye. She looked away and said, "It's nothing . . . I can handle this."

Arlene persisted. "Don't tell me that those marks are from Marcus. Are they? Look at me and tell me the truth."

"Okay," Jessica sighed. "Marcus gets a little out of control sometimes, and I bruise easily. He is always sorry and promises not to be so rough again."

Arlene knew her friend needed help. Marcus was physically abusing Jessica.

Arlene put her arms around Jessica and told her that physical abuse is never right. She assured Jessica that she should never think she did something wrong to deserve the abuse.

"I am glad you told me about this," Arlene said. "There is a hotline number we can call after school. They will give us advice on how to handle this. We are also going to tell your parents. I will be there with you."

Aggression in Dating and Relationships

Aggression in dating can be physical or verbal. Research indicates that incidences of dating aggression are high and that large numbers of teenagers are at risk for serious injury. Physical aggression that occurs while dating or in a relationship may include pushing, slapping, punching, choking, or threatening someone with bodily harm.

Verbal aggression may include criticism, ridicule, shouting, ignoring, name-calling, humiliation, and not being allowed to make your own decisions or speak when you want to do so.

Date rape is a specific and extreme type of aggression. Many people think only strangers commit rapes; however, the majority of rape survivors have been raped by people they know. Exact numbers of date rapes are hard to determine because many rapes are never reported. Rape is a violent crime and is never the victim's fault. It should be reported to the police, and the survivor should seek medical and psychological help.

Sometimes it is difficult to recognize the signs of an abusive relationship. Learning how to recognize and be aware of these aggressive behaviors is important. Teenagers in dating relationships where one partner acts aggressively toward another may feel hopeless and helpless. However, it is vital to remember that help is always available.

Look at the Where to Go for Help section at the back of this book to find listings of associations you can contact for more information. If you or someone you know is in immediate danger, call 911 and ask the police for help. Otherwise, call a hotline, join a support group, or contact a close friend, relative, favorite teacher, or other trusted adult and ask for help.

Road Rage

When you are driving and another driver cuts you off, follows you too closely, flashes lights, honks at you, or yells obscenities, he or she is an aggressive driver.

Aggressive driving, also known as road rage, has increased throughout the United States in recent years. Identifying and preventing road rage is especially important for adolescents because of the high statistics for injuries and deaths in this age group.

According to the CDC, the current leading cause of death among young people ages ten to twenty-four is motor vehicle accidents. The National Highway Transportation Safety Administration estimates that angry drivers have been responsible for 2.28 million crashes and 27,935 traffic fatalities in the past five years. Research shows that teenagers are more likely than older drivers to speed, run lights, make illegal turns, ride with an intoxicated driver, and drive after using alcohol and drugs. They are also more likely to underestimate the potential dangers in hazardous situations and have less experience coping with them. As we have already seen, aggressive behaviors are often considered unlawful behaviors. From vandalism to date rape to road rage, aggression hurts. Again, if you have trouble controlling your behavior or know someone who does, seek assistance before things get really out of control.

Schools and Aggression

Katrina, fourteen, was the new girl in school. Katrina could not speak English. Her family had arrived recently from Russia.

On the first day of class, Erica, another freshman, smiled at the new girl and invited her to sit with Erica at lunch. Erica learned that Katrina lived in her neighborhood and was riding on the same school bus. The two tried carrying on a conversation, but Katrina was mostly smiling and nodding her head.

Leonard was a junior who always hogged the backseat of the bus. From there, he would make comments about everyone who got on. Some students turned up the volume on their CD players so the music from their headphones would drown out his comments; others would just ignore him. But he seemed to get pleasure from bullying and embarrassing Katrina.

Whenever Katrina got on the bus, Leonard would say, "Here comes the cow . . . moo, moo, moo."

Katrina knew he was making fun of her, even though she didn't always understand everything he was saying. Erica did not know what to say or do, so she kept silent. She felt really bad for Katrina, and she hated watching the tears well up in her friend's eyes.

One day, some other immature boys on the bus joined in the mooing. Erica knew this was horrible but did not know what to do. The bullying had gone too far.

Katrina was absent the next day. Leonard went up to Erica and said, "Where's moo-moo today? Out in the pasture?"

Erica looked directly at Leonard and told him that he was a jerk and that he wasn't funny at all. Then she looked around at the others and said, "Anyone else have anything mean to say?"

Everyone just kind of shook their heads, and all of a sudden seemed intent on burying their faces in their notebooks. Leonard mumbled something about Erica liking "moo-moo" too much. Then he slunk back to to the rear of the bus.

Later that day, Erica visited the principal, Mr. August. She felt terrible about Katrina—she was sure that Katrina wasn't sick and that she was staying at home because she didn't want to deal with Leonard. She thought that Mr. August would be able to do something about Leonard's behavior. She was right.

Mr. August said that this form of aggression would not be tolerated. It was bad for the victim and bad for those who witnessed the bullying. He spoke privately

*to Leonard and met with Katrina the following day.
Mr. August suspended Leonard for a week and asked
that Leonard apologize to Katrina.*

*Eventually, the student council led a schoolwide
campaign aimed at promoting tolerance and positive
social behaviors.*

As institutions, schools often reflect and dramatize
social problems. While schools teach students facts and
figures, they are also sites where a large number of young
people come together and interact socially. When acts of
violence and aggression occur between students in school,
it is important for school officials to address the behavior.
If these antisocial, aggressive acts are not punished, other
students may imitate these behaviors. All students need to
see that aggressive behavior in school is punished. This is
true in cases of both verbal and physical aggression.

The Safe and Drug-Free Schools Program

Nonviolent ways of coping with aggression need to be
taught and practiced. The Safe and Drug-Free Schools and
Communities Act was passed in 1987. It was enacted to
prevent the illegal use of alcohol, tobacco, and drugs. In
1994, the act was reauthorized and extended to prevent
violence as well as illicit drug use. This act is the federal
government's primary vehicle for reducing violence
through educational and preventative activities.

The act allows state and local governments to apply for
and receive funds to undertake a broad range of drug and
violence prevention strategies. The money can be used to
purchase instructional materials, implement counseling

services, purchase metal detectors, hire security guards, and implement before- and after-school recreational, instructional, cultural, and/or artistic programs. More school policies and programs against aggression are needed to provide safe environments.

School Security Measures
Recent tragic events such as school shootings have prompted teachers and school administrators to examine school safety and aggression. The U.S. Department of Education lists the following percentage of public schools that in 1998 used various security measures to combat the dangers of aggressive students.

↪ Daily metal detector checks—1 percent

↪ Random metal detector checks—4 percent

↪ Drug sweeps—19 percent

↪ Controlled access to school grounds—24 percent

↪ Controlled access to school buildings—53 percent

↪ Closed campus during lunch—80 percent

↪ Visitors must sign in—96 percent

Warning Signs of Potentially Violent Students

As student aggression is often linked to rejection experienced in the classroom, it is neither useful nor wise to label students prematurely as "bad" or "problematic."

A more fruitful approach is to be aware of traits that may indicate that a student has the potential to be outwardly aggressive. While it is unfortunate that all schools are not necessarily safe for students, it is important to confront the problem and work together toward a solution. The National Association of School Psychologists has developed a list of warning signs to alert school personnel to potentially violent students who may exhibit or complain of the following:

➩ Excessive feelings of isolation

➩ Social withdrawal

➩ Excessive feelings of rejection

➩ Being a victim of violence

➩ Feelings of being picked on and/or persecuted

➩ Decreased interest in school and poor academic performance or falling grades

➩ Expressions of violence in writings and drawings

➩ Uncontrolled anger

➩ Patterns of intimidating and bullying behaviors

➩ History of discipline problems

➩ Past history of violent and aggressive behavior

➩ Intolerance of differences and prejudicial attitudes

 Drug and alcohol use

 Inappropriate access to, possession of, and/or use of firearms

 Serious threats of violence

Witnessing someone being bullied can have a long-term effect on a person. Witnesses should take some action, either by getting help directly or anonymously, standing up to a bully, or empathizing with the victim. Many people simply walk away from a bullying scene just to avoid giving the bully an audience. If you find yourself confronted by a bully at school, or you think you have the potential to bully someone, please seek adult assistance.

Sports and Aggression

The football team at Central High School was upset about the rumored behavior of football players at other schools. There were reports in the local news of jocks being bullies, abusing their classmates, fighting at events, being physically aggressive with girls, not doing classwork, and even getting into trouble with the law.

Coach Lyman always held his team up to high standards. He considered good grades, teamwork, discipline, and a positive attitude to be important parts of being an athlete.

One day after practice, some players decided to go out for pizza. Jared was driving four of the other guys. He pressed every button on the car radio but could not find any station he liked. It was time for the hourly news.

What they heard angered them.

"Breaking news: Four high school football players have been accused of sexually assaulting a mentally impaired girl," stated the announcer.

"Why does it always have to be jocks?" said Seth.

They all wondered how long it would take for someone to ask, "Do things like that happen around here, too?"

Seth, Jared, and the others began kicking around ideas about how to resolve the problem of aggressive and violent jocks.

Mike suggested, "Let's talk to Mr. Domino, our athletic director. Maybe we can unite all the school's athletes and try to figure out a way to stop the violence."

Seth continued, "I know soccer players who feel the same way. We need to promote the fact that we have good morals and values, and we want to stop hot-headed, self-centered jerks and perverts."

Several players met with Mr. Domino and decided to have a meeting to educate others about sports rage.

"Sometimes tragedies provide opportunities," said Mr. Domino. "We are organizing information forums for students, staff, and parents."

The school project was extended to educate the community about high school sports. Brochures and posters were designed to describe the high standards set for athletes and to ask for community support. The results were very positive. Attendance at athletic events increased and more pride was felt throughout the school.

Athletic competitions can motivate a person to achieve his or her personal best. For some teenagers, sports promote personal well-being, improve individual physical and social skills, and develop a lifelong healthy interest in exercise. Unfortunately, there is evidence that suggests that sports can also produce anxiety and aggression, and this aggression can be a problem for players, coaches, parents, and fans.

Sports Rage

Sports rage occurs when families, coaches, and spectators are out of control at sporting events. Consider the following examples.

- ↪ Two fathers fight during a hockey game. One father attacks the other while their children watch.

- ↪ A foul is called during a soccer game. A coach attacks the referee and breaks his nose.

Witnessing parents, coaches, or other adults becoming violent during sporting events has severe detrimental implications for youth and the whole of society.

Some researchers feel that sports aggression is a learned behavior. As previously mentioned, according to social learning theory, aggression is a learned behavior. As such, if the behavior is rewarded, it will be repeated. Watching peers, older students, or professional athletes use harmful aggression on and off the field and later be praised for that behavior enables the behavior to be imitated. Positive reinforcement may often be provided by coaches, teammates, family, friends, and the media.

It has been reported that the two boys responsible for the Columbine High School massacre in Littleton, Colorado, on April 20, 1999, were angered and preoccupied by the treatment of athletes at their high school. It is reported that some athletes were allowed to play in games even though several were bullies. At the beginning of their bloody rampage, the killers reportedly targeted athletes. At the end of it all, thirteen people were killed and twenty-one were wounded. The two perpetrators committed suicide by shooting themselves at the scene.

Anabolic Steroids

Aggression in sports is also linked to the use of anabolic steroids. The National Institute on Drug Abuse reports that about half a million adolescents are using anabolic steroids. Anabolic steroids are synthetic compounds that mimic the action of male hormones. Doctors use these drugs to treat delayed puberty or to treat those who are suffering from an advanced stage of acquired immunodeficiency syndrome (AIDS). High doses of anabolic steroids are used by some athletes to increase muscle mass and improve performance. High doses taken by abusers are up to one hundred times greater than doses used for treating medical conditions. These high doses can lead to depression, hostility, and aggression. Sometimes this is referred to as "roid rage." The following is a list of side effects of anabolic steroid use.

➸ Aggression

➸ Heart disease

⇀ Kidney cancer

⇀ Liver cancer

⇀ Eating disorders

⇀ Stunted growth

⇀ Acne

Anabolic steroids can be taken orally, by injection, or through creams or gels that are rubbed onto the skin. The use of unsterilized needles also poses a risk for various infections, including the human immunodeficiency virus (HIV), which causes AIDS. If you use steroids, you should stop and, if necessary, seek help. If you know someone who uses steroids, talk to that person and make sure that he or she is aware of the potential dangers involved.

What to Remember

The object of team sports is not to win at all costs but to learn sportsmanship, self-control, and self-discipline. Instead of getting angry and aggressive after losing, adolescents should be reminded that losing and mistakes are part of life. The emphasis in athletics should be on developing skills, teamwork, respect for others, self-respect, and accepting defeat graciously.

What Is Coping?

Learning how to control aggression will enable you to have more success in school, foster healthy personal relationships, and ultimately help you get the most out of life. Many psychologists feel that aggression is one of the strongest predictors of delinquency and antisocial behavior. Interestingly, some researchers feel that, as youths mature, over time they learn how to control their anger and prevent aggressive episodes. Regardless, learning and practicing productive and healthy coping strategies is a good idea.

Basic Coping Strategies

An inability to cope with stress, disappointment, and adversity can affect your life in many negative ways: physically, psychologically, and socially. Adolescence can be stressful. Physical changes in your body, academic demands, peer pressure, learning how to deal with cliques, family problems, and concerns about the future may become stressors. Learning how to control your emotions and behavior and take responsibility for them is a lifelong process. However, it is best to start as soon as possible.

Successful coping may involve one of many strategies: positive thinking, problem solving, logical thinking, spiritual or social support, engaging in a creative or athletic activity, or seeking professional help. People cope differently, and what works best for one person may not be the best, most effective strategy or method for someone else. Your method of coping may vary according to the situation. You may handle a situation at home differently than you would at school. There is no one formula for effective coping that can be used at all times and in all situations.

You will learn coping skills throughout your entire life. They must be practiced, adjusted, and broadened. Your life will be enriched if you have a wide repertoire of how to cope in different situations. In AD 65, Seneca, a Roman philosopher, wrote about anger and aggression and recommended the following strategies, which are still useful in modern times.

- Avoid frustrating situations by noting when you became angry in the past.

- Reduce your anger by taking time to think things through.

- Respond calmly to an aggressor with empathy, or ignore him or her.

☞Think about the undesirable consequences of becoming angry.

☞Reconsider the circumstances and try to understand the motives of the other person.

☞Be tolerant and forgiving of human weakness.

These strategies were not based on formal scientific research but on anecdotal evidence and studies. Even after all these years, these strategies are still relevant and effective.

Problem Solving

Situations can be viewed as opportunities rather than problems. When you make rational decisions, you are coping rather than being impulsive and allowing your anger to escalate to the point that it may lead to aggression. Life is a series of decisions. Try to think of problem solving as decision making. When you believe that something poses a problem, use the same steps you would take if you were making any decision. These steps typically involve assessing the situation, defining the problem, implementing a solution, and evaluating the results.

Conflict Resolution

Conflict resolution is a term you may have heard in school or during community meetings. Conflict resolution teaches young people how to manage conflict and provides them with lifelong decision-making skills. Conflict resolution involves bringing people in a dispute together to identify their interests, express their views, and seek mutually acceptable solutions. In fact, some schools teach conflict resolution in classes as part of the curriculum. If you are involved in a dispute, here are some guidelines for resolving conflicts.

- Ask the other person involved in the dispute if he or she has time to talk.

- Control your emotions and be relaxed.

- Identify the facts concerning the conflict.

- Use "I am feeling . . ." statements. For example, if you are arguing with someone who repeatedly interrupts you, say "I am feeling frustrated because I cannot finish my sentences."

- Listen to the other person.

- Discuss ways to resolve the conflict at hand.

- Think about a solution.

- Settle upon a mutual agreement or agree to leave and discuss the conflict at a later time.

Sometimes conflicts cannot be resolved. If this is the case, it is important to respect other people's differences without causing further anger or aggression.

Reducing Stress

Stress often leads to anger and aggression. Learning how to reduce stress will improve your ability to cope. There are many activities that reduce stress, including getting enough sleep, regular exercise, eating nutritious meals, and avoiding nicotine, caffeine, and sweets.

In order to reduce stress, you need to prioritize your activities. You will need to decide what you can control and what you have no control over. You may find that you are involved in too many activities, or you may need to address a habit of procrastinating when faced with responsibilities.

Sometimes you may need to seek out a quiet space to be alone or meditate. You might listen to calming music or take a bath. At other times, it may help to visit with friends or go see a funny movie. You might also start trying to be more tolerant of others and refrain from judging them.

Learning How to Relax

Incorporating relaxation techniques into your life can help reduce stress. However, relaxation techniques do require discipline. It helps to practice at the same time every day. Some simple suggestions include:

➣ **Focused breathing.** Paying attention to your breathing can calm you. Inhale through your nose, count to four, and feel the cool air as it hits the back of your throat. Picture the air entering your lungs. Pause for a second, and exhale to a count of four. Feel the warm air leave your nose. Repeat.

56

↝ **Visualization and guided imagery.** This activity uses all of your senses in thinking about a pleasant scene. It can be a real place or just imagined. For example, if you think of a beach, try to smell the salt water, feel the hot sun, and imagine that you can hear the sound of the waves crashing onto the shore.

↝ **Progressive muscle relaxation.** Begin by tensing and then relaxing all the muscle groups in your body. Begin with your toes and work up to your head, tensing and releasing as you work your way up.

Another relaxation technique that you can use just about anywhere is to repeat a calm word or phrase slowly—many people pray or like to repeat a favorite religious phrase. Even if you aren't religious, it can be relaxing to think of a favorite saying or line of poetry, and repeat it to yourself while breathing slowly and deeply.

Assertiveness

Whether you are trying to modify your own aggressive impulses or you are dealing with the aggressive behavior of others, developing assertiveness skills is a great idea. Developing assertiveness skills decreases a person's feelings of anger and, consequently, acts of aggression. Being assertive means acting and speaking in a calm yet direct and forthright manner. If teens feel that they have calmly and clearly stood up for themselves and expressed their feelings, they should feel less frustrated. It is also important to remember that other people should also feel they can communicate assertively.

Role Playing: Practicing Assertiveness

It is sometimes helpful to practice assertive responses before actually using them. This will help you become more confident in your ability to be assertive. Role playing with a friend or in a group can also be great practice. It is important to remember that no one is born with these skills. While it is certainly difficult to deal with aggressive groups, avoiding these situations may not work. And, while assertiveness can definitely help, it won't always be an option. It's part of a solution to a larger problem. In the end, it's up to families, schools, and the community to work together and do some problem solving that will hopefully reduce the incidences of teenage aggression.

When Being Assertive Succeeds: Cathy's Story

Cathy needed some new shirts. She went to the mall on Saturday, but she had to rush since she had a baby-sitting job later that afternoon. She didn't think that she had enough time to try on all the shirts that interested her, but she did try on a few of them. At any rate, since they were all the same brand, she figured it would be fine if she didn't try everything on—and she couldn't refuse, since they were on sale and the price was great.

It wasn't until later the next day, on Sunday, that Cathy had the time to empty out her shopping bags and hang up her purchases. While doing so, she noticed that a thread was pulled on the green top.

She looked at it more closely and saw that there was a small hole where the thread was sticking out from the fabric. Immediately, she put on her coat to head back to the store and ask for a refund.

Once at the store, Cathy walked up to a salesperson and said, "I would like a refund for this top."

The salesperson responded, "I need to see the receipt and the garment."

Cathy handed over her bag and the salesperson looked carefully at the top and said, "You bought it this way? You didn't notice this? This is why the top was reduced."

Looking directly at the salesperson, Cathy calmly said, "There is nothing stated about a final sale and I would like a refund."

The salesperson appeared to be annoyed and took another approach. "How could you buy something with a hole like this—could it have happened after you bought it?"

Standing tall, taking a deep breath, and speaking directly to the woman, Cathy repeated, "I purchased this top yesterday. It has a defect. I have my receipt, and I want my money back."

The salesperson finally gave in. She went over to the cash register and started counting out the money to refund to Cathy.

This situation worked out in Cathy's favor because she stood up for herself—she was assertive. She didn't get angry, she didn't raise her voice, and she maintained self-control. Because of this, she was able to get what she rightly deserved.

Self-Efficacy

The belief that you are capable of exercising some control over your life and that you are capable of realizing your goals is called perceived self-efficacy. People who believe that they can manage situations are often less distressed than those who face difficult or new situations with fear and a premature sense of defeat. People with successful coping abilities tend to have better control over their thoughts, are able to ask for support from others, and tend to be more optimistic than those individuals who lack coping strategies.

As discussed earlier, bullies are often controlling and aggressive. However, a person with high self-efficacy is able to cope without resorting to aggression and is resilient under stress. According to the American Psychological Association, resiliency—the sense of self-preservation that helps counter negative effects of stress—can be developed.

An assertive person faces problems promptly and focuses on solutions rather than on difficulties. Practicing assertiveness skills will promote self-efficacy and increase your ability to cope.

Communicating

There is a difference between communicating aggressively and communicating assertively. An aggressive person may express himself or herself by:

⇝ Yelling or screaming

⇝ Using abusive or disrespectful language

➲ Becoming threatening or physically abusive

➲ Concealing feelings until he or she explodes

Contrastingly, an assertive person remains calm, speaks respectfully, and explains how he or she feels by using "I" statements. Using "I" messages is important when communicating assertively with others. An "I" statement describes how you feel. For example, "I feel hurt when I am criticized in front of others." Using "I" statements helps us recognize and express our emotions without accusing the other person of intentionally causing them.

Active Listening

Active listening is also an essential part of effective communication. Active listening gives a listener the sense that you want to understand his or her point of view. Understanding does not mean that you agree with what is being said but that you respect the other person's perspective. Saying things like "I would like to hear what you think about . . . " or "Could you tell me what you think about . . . " shows that you respect the other person's views.

Empathy, or understanding, is crucial to active listening and fruitful interactions with others. Some people seem more readily empathetic and can quickly read another person's emotions through his or her facial expressions and gestures. The empathetic person is able to put himself or herself in the other person's shoes. Some people are naturally empathetic, while others need to practice it like a skill. Empathizing means you are trying to understand another person's feelings or circumstances. It helps reduce conflict because it increases understanding and acceptance. Listening and empathizing can defuse anger and aggression.

Nonverbal communication is also another important part of active listening. Looking directly at the other person or persons with whom you are communicating suggests that you are listening in an attentive fashion. You can verify whether or not you are accurately understanding the intended meaning of what is being said by asking questions like "I heard you say . . . Did I understand you correctly?" or "Is this what you mean?"

Do you appear to be paying attention to the person to whom you are speaking, or are you distracted by the television, watching the clock, or walking away? When you are with someone, your eye contact, facial expressions, posture, and gestures can convey a great deal. Nonverbal behaviors are often harder to control than verbal behaviors, but they can be modified through self-awareness and practice. The following is a list of nonverbal behaviors that facilitate self-assertion and positive communication with others.

➥ **Eye contact.** Look directly at the person you are speaking with and focus on his or her eyes. Maintaining eye contact shows you are listening.

➥ **Posture.** A relaxed posture communicates confidence and self-control. However, an overly relaxed posture is often equated with inattentiveness, disinterest, and even defiance.

➯**Facial expressions.** Your face can reveal your emotions and signal if you are interested, alert, or in agreement.

➯**Gestures.** Use hand gestures to emphasize what you are saying and try to avoid fidgeting.

➯**Tone of voice.** Speak clearly and loudly enough so that you can be heard by those with whom you are communicating. Do not yell or whisper.

Developing assertiveness and active listening skills will make it easier for you to speak up and ask for things, to express your negative and positive emotions, to question things, and to share feelings, opinions, and experiences. It will also give you the strength and energy to listen to and understand others.

Confronting Aggression

Teenagers often experience conflicts with peers and authority figures, such as parents or teachers. Confronting aggression in your life may involve getting help if you are the aggressive individual. At times, it may be difficult to distinguish between rebellious activities that are a positive form of self-assertion (and adolescent identity formation) and aggression. However, if a consistent pattern of destructive anger and aggressive behavior develops, it would be wise to address it. One of the first steps in dealing with aggressive behaviors is to look for a cause—and doing so usually requires a visit to a counselor or a medical doctor.

The first step is to seek professional help. A medical doctor may perform a physical examination and recommend further testing in order to make an accurate diagnosis. The doctor may suggest treating aggressive behavior with medication and/or counseling and behavioral interventions.

Medication

Sometimes aggressive behavior stems from a physical or chemical problem. Medication may be prescribed to correct an imbalance of chemicals in the brain. Brain chemicals are called neurotransmitters. There are more than forty different neurotransmitters that influence our emotions and behaviors. One such neurotransmitter is serotonin. Serotonin is involved in the inhibition of impulsivity. Prescription stimulants can increase levels of serotonin. An example of one such drug is Ritalin (methylphenidate).

Sometimes aggression is associated with depression. In this case, a doctor might prescribe an antidepressant. In other instances, a mood stabilizer such as lithium carbonate might reduce aggression. For some individuals, an antipsychotic medication such as thorazine may become necessary. While medication is effective in some cases, it is important to remember that medication need not be the first or only option for treating aggression. Family support services, educational classes, and counseling are examples of other approaches to dealing with aggression.

Counseling

Many professionals, such as psychiatric social workers, nurse clinical specialists, psychologists, and psychiatrists counsel people who are struggling with aggressive tendencies. Psychiatrists are medical doctors who are licensed to prescribe medication. Psychologists, nurses, and social workers may have doctorate degrees in their specialty area, but they are not medical doctors. Spiritual or religious leaders are also often consulted for counseling.

Behavioral Intervention

In some cases, ongoing counseling for an aggressive teen and his or her family may be necessary. A counseling plan may also include training in various skills such as problem solving and assertiveness. In extreme cases of uncontrollable aggression, hospitalization is often required.

Confronting Aggression

Bullies can be physically aggressive, and as we saw with Katrina and Erica in chapter 5, bullies who are verbally aggressive are also extremely hurtful. The following are ways to keep bullies at bay.

- Do not let someone force you into a physical fight.

- If someone insults you, it is important that you realize that he or she is trying to anger you.

- If someone insults a person you care about, remember that he or she is just trying to upset you.

- If someone confronts you physically, back away to protect yourself.

- Never carry a weapon. Although you may be carrying it for protection, you are endangering yourself and others.

- Whenever possible, avoid gangs and bullies.

- Be assertive and say things like "Leave me alone, or I will tell the teacher (the coach, my parents, or the police)."

➥ If you absolutely must walk or be in the vicinity of bullies or other aggressive people, don't go alone. Have a family member, a friend, or even a group of friends accompany you.

➥ If a bully has bothered you, contact school officials or counselors. They can confront the bully and demand that he or she stop bothering you.

➥ Practice the assertiveness skills discussed in the previous chapter.

➥ If someone is seriously threatening you, protect yourself immediately. Leave him or her alone because it is unsafe to be near him or her. Call friends, family, or the police for help.

Dealing Successfully with Angry People

If you find yourself confronted by an angry person, try some of these suggestions from the Institute of Mental Health Initiatives.

➥ Try to stay calm.

➥ Acknowledge that the other person is angry.

➥ Ask the angry person to explain the situation.

➥ Listen without interrupting or judging.

➥ Explain your feelings using "I" statements. For example, "I'd like to work this out, but I'll have to get help if you can't control yourself."

Take Action

We are all well aware that school bullies can cause serious problems for people. If bullies get away with aggressive behavior, they are more likely to go on hurting others. The Violence Institute of New Jersey recommends a comprehensive approach when responding to school bullying. They advise school officials to observe the following guidelines.

- Establish schoolwide policies and procedures for dealing with bullies.

- Provide training for school personnel.

- Have classroom discussions about these issues.

- Implement social skills training programs and classroom based curricula.

- Provide enhanced adult supervision of places where bullies hang out.

- Arrange family meetings and family counseling.

- Provide counseling or access to counseling for victims, bullies, and bystanders.

- Have procedures in place that will facilitate an ongoing statistical account of instances of bullying and an assessment of attitudes toward bullies in the school.

Your Actions Are Important

If you start feeling unsafe at school, it is important to talk to a trusted adult. You may be the first to recognize serious warning signs of aggression in others that could ultimately lead to violence. Therefore, voicing your concerns could mean the difference between life and death. If you notice someone exhibiting the following behaviors, share your concerns with a teacher, guidance counselor, school nurse, or principal.

↪ Bully or threaten other people

↪ Exhibit cruelty to pets or other animals

↪ Carry a weapon

↪ Display an obsession with violent films or games

It is important to cultivate a respectful attitude toward others and to practice nonaggressive responses in problem solving with your schoolmates and peers. There are several things you can do. Form peer groups to address concerns about aggressive behaviors, and speak out against aggression in music, in movies, in video games, and on television. Meet with your school administrators and point out ways to reduce opportunities and rewards for bullying behaviors. Join school committees to address schoolwide practices of discipline, curriculum content, and building stronger connections as a community. Establish an anonymous hotline that will enable students to share their concerns safely about their aggressive tendencies or about aggression they have witnessed in others. Suggest "Aggression-free" days and rallies and develop plans to commit to stopping aggression.

Through strong leadership, a caring faculty, parent involvement, and student participation, communities can design programs and policies that will ensure that schools are safe places.

Working Together: A Great Solution

Bill, sixteen, was always in trouble—even when he was in elementary school. He didn't care about all of the problems that he caused, especially since his mother was usually on his side.

Bill's mom always defended his behavior and told everyone: "Stop picking on my son."

If Bill wanted someone's lunch, he'd take it. His classmates feared him and would never report his wrongdoings for fear of being beaten up. He never smiled and was hostile toward his teachers and other students. He had no friends—at least none that anyone at school ever saw. Rumor had it that he hung out with an older gang that was suspected of committing local robberies.

"Open the door for me, freak," Bill ordered a young, timid freshman who was carrying an armful of books.

The kid looked at Bill and froze.

"What's wrong, dog-face—you deaf or something?" Bill roared.

The kid didn't move. After two seconds, Bill lunged toward the younger kid and shoved him to the ground. It just so happened that a school security guard was walking by, and the next thing Bill knew, he was being escorted to the main office.

In the office, the security guard frisked Bill and found out that he was carrying a gun.

Bill was expelled.

The student council was appalled. They believed that no one in their school should be bullied or made to feel threatened or unsafe. Representatives met with the disciplinary committee and the parent-teacher organization. The group was determined to stop aggression and promote school pride.

An assembly was planned to address concerns, discuss a plan of action, and rally for school support. The school newspaper ran informational pieces about the causes of aggression and articles on ways to cope. Local psychologists organized several lectures on anger management and methods of dealing with an aggressive child for parents with children of all ages— even those with preschoolers.

Students, staff, and parents all devoted themselves to confronting and coping with aggression.

Focus on Family and Community

As discussed in chapter 3, many people believe that violence and aggression are often learned behaviors. Children of angry and abusive parents may become angry and abusive adults. Because of this, communities need to be aware of child abuse and must work at developing strategies that enable prevention of all forms of child abuse—be it verbal, sexual, or physical.

Aggressive children often grow into aggressive teens. It is not easy to determine when aggressive or violently explosive behavior is sufficiently disruptive to seek professional help. Also, many parents simply do not know how to control a child's behavior. Physically punishing a young child or ignoring aggressive behavior are both ineffective and often harmful strategies. Harsh physical discipline can enrage children. This rage can remain repressed but may be released later by exerting control over others.

Discipline

Discipline is not punishment. The word "discipline" comes from the Latin word *disciplina*, meaning "instruction" or "teaching." Building relationships on trust, having appropriate expectations, setting limits, offering praise, and implementing logical and reasonable consequences for misbehavior can help address a child's aggressive tendencies. Effective discipline treats children with respect while shaping their behavior to encourage self-control and respect for others.

Children have a right to feel angry, but aggressive behaviors are not to be ignored or tolerated. Aggressive acts can accelerate from minor to serious offenses. Parents may need to seek professional advice on how to discipline their kids, and how to prevent, recognize, and respond to aggression.

Keep the Paths of Communication Open

Many things, such as dealing with a divorce, a job loss, an illness, or a death, can put families under a lot of pressure. During particularly stressful times, a family may benefit from counseling. Counseling may help ease the transition to the next phase of life. Also during these periods, teens may need more attention from their parents. At times like these, it is essential to maintain open and healthy lines of communication. It is important to ask each other questions about how each of you are feeling and try to listen without interrupting. Teens may feel lost and frightened and need to talk about tensions at home. In such cases, speaking to a mentor or school adviser may prove helpful.

Community Involvement

Teens benefit from personal attention and structured, predictable environments. After-school mentoring, tutoring, and work or volunteer programs should be available for teens so they can learn important skills, form valuable relationships, and earn income. Programs that promote physical and mental health are also needed. Access to transportation to these programs, in addition to libraries and sports facilities, must be available. Youth forums with community and church leaders and law enforcement agents can provide teens with an opportunity to express concerns and build working relationships.

The National Campaign Against Youth Violence has launched a national public awareness effort to change the way Americans think about and address youth violence. Teens themselves are taking a stand against aggression. SHINE (Seeking Harmony in Neighborhoods Everyday) is a youth service organization that uses outlets such as music, art, and technology to enhance communities. The group's members work to end violence, organize mentoring and peer mediation programs, and teach conflict resolution and anger management. The group's Web site is www.shine.excite.com.

There are clubs and associations throughout the United States and in Canada that can assist teens with developing problem-solving skills, promoting self-esteem, building friendships, and finding positive role models. Youth groups such as Big Brothers Big Sisters (in the U.S.) and Big Brothers and Big Sisters (in Canada) and other associations offer respectful guidance and teach effective strategies on how to maintain healthy relationships. Sometimes all you need is someone to listen. Take a look at the Where to Go for Help section at the back of this book for listings of organizations that can help.

New Legislation

Teen advocacy extends beyond family, schools, and communities. State and federal public policies may need to be introduced to address aggression and violence in society. Legislation regarding gun control and weapons is also needed.

Drug abuse problems need to be addressed as well. Research has shown that adolescents who are involved in constructive, adult-supervised activities outside of school are less likely to use drugs. Drug abuse is often associated with a variety of negative consequences, such as violent behavior, school failure, legal troubles, and automobile accidents. As discussed in chapter 4, aggression is often expressed while driving. If you meet up with an aggressive driver, some helpful points to remember are:

➭ Be cautious. Every situation is a potential danger.

➭ Stay calm. Do not react to anger with anger.

➭ Avoid the person and focus on safe driving. Back away and avoid violence.

➭ Seek help. Call for help and report the driver to the authorities; you may eliminate other incidents of aggressive driving.

Presently, several agencies, including the Centers for Disease Control and Prevention, the National Center for Injury Prevention and Control, and the National Institutes of Health are evaluating various attempts to reduce aggressive driving, control anger, and reduce the number of crashes. Many states have passed laws to identify aggressive drivers, revoke their licenses, and impose fines for aggressive driving.

Transcending Anger and Aggression

Recognizing your anger and controlling it can lead to better overall health and the prevention of aggression. In learning to control anger, you must identify your triggers. What makes you angry? Are you being annoyed, insulted, or falsely accused? Recognize these triggers and prepare yourself for a situation with positive thinking. Say things to yourself such as "I know I can manage this," "this may be difficult, but I can control my anger," "I believe in myself," and "I can do this."

It also helps to try to be aware of your physical reactions to anger. Do you clench your fists or start to sweat, or does your heart beat faster? When you feel your muscles starting to tense, take a deep breath and tell yourself to stay calm. Try to think clearly and remember that you cannot control other people but that you can control what you say and do. Tell yourself that getting upset will not help—as long as you keep calm, you are in control and capable of handling the situation.

Developing a tolerance of others can reduce your anger and aggression. By understanding the feelings, actions, and motivations of other people, you may become more accepting of them, even if you disagree with their beliefs. This is the general philosophy behind tolerance training and one of the foundations of several religions. Just as Christians are taught to "turn the other cheek," you should try to practice tolerance with others as well.

Forgiving is not forgetting, but it is a decision to no longer hate or feel angry. Amazing and powerful people who helped bring about important social changes, such as Mahatma Gandhi and the Rev. Dr. Martin Luther King Jr., advocated nonviolent approaches to dealing with those who opposed them.

Problem Solving

You may not be able to solve all problems, but the following problem-solving steps will guide you.

➾ Identify the problem.

➾ List the causes.

➾ Think about solutions.

➾ Plan a solution.

➾ Implement the solution.

➾ Evaluate the results.

A Good Approach: Feeling Angry and Moving On

Shinita was livid. She thought that Todd was acting weird when they had gone to the movies last Saturday. After the show, Todd had felt tired, and he drove her straight home. When she phoned him the next day, he said that he was tired and planned to rest the entire day.

"What's up, dude?" quizzed Shinita.

"I think I'm coming down with something," Todd replied. "I'm going to just hang out the whole day."

"Want company?" asked Shinita.

"No, I think I'm just going to hit the sack. I'm not feeling like company," moaned Todd.

Shinita, a cheerleader, went ahead and made plans with some of her teammates to watch a football game being played by one their school's rival teams. They were curious about the performance of the team's cheerleaders, and it would be great to hang out with friends.

Later on that day, the friends climbed into the stands at the fifty-yard line. They had a great view of the playing field and the crowd. In fact, their view was too good. There, midway down toward the left thirty-yard line, was Todd—with his arm around some girl! Shinita felt like running down and hitting him and pulling out the girl's hair!

"Wow! Oh, my God!" yelled Shinita.

The others couldn't believe their eyes. Shinita was hurt, confused, and angry.

"I can't believe he lied to me!" she cried.

The girls gave Shinita their support.

Marisa said, "You deserve better."

Cheryl suggested that they all march down to say hello to the two-timer, and they encouraged Shinita to hold her head up high. They rehearsed exactly what they would say and how they would proceed.

Shinita took several deep breaths. She felt more calm and focused. She told herself that she would not overreact. She realized that she and Todd were never really "a couple." She knew she would have to get over this; she did not want to waste her time on a guy like him. She imagined herself getting through the situation successfully.

Todd was shocked to be greeted by Shinita and her friends. There was no scene, just unemotional hellos. Todd seemed pretty embarrassed and uncomfortable around them.

The girls exited the stadium and headed for the nearest diner. They congratulated Shinita for being strong and urged her not to think about Todd.

Shinita felt optimistic about going out with other guys and was grateful for the support of her friends.

Having supportive friends, learning how to analyze a situation logically, and rehearsing how you are going to act and what you are going to say are important ways of dealing with anger and aggression. It is also important to recognize when you have succeeded in improving your coping skills. After you have responded calmly to an anger-inducing situation, remember to tell yourself that you did a good job and mentally give yourself a pat on the back. Remind yourself that you are getting better all the time.

Small Changes Go a Long Way

The following are seemingly small yet enormously helpful ways of not becoming tangled in tense situations.

- Remember to laugh. Laughter relieves physical stress, and humor can help you gain a new perspective.

- Change your environment by briefly leaving the site of the conflict. Spend some time quietly by yourself. If you are stuck indoors, try stretching all your muscles—your back, arms, neck, shoulders, and legs.

- Avoid stimulants like caffeine and nicotine; they can make you more jumpy, anxious, and fearful.

- Drink lots of water and tell yourself that you are on a journey to improve your health.

- Avoid loud noise when you are irritable; soothing music can relieve stress.

- Exercise regularly; it benefits both your body and mind.

- Try to be flexible and give in occasionally; you do not always have to know everything or always be right. Let go of the small annoyances and let go of the things you cannot change.

- Instead of looking at something as a problem, consider it a challenge.

- Spend less time with your angry friends and more time with those who are calm and congenial.

➡ Make an effort to avoid put-downs; aggressive remarks hurt others and harm relationships.

➡ Consider what is the right thing to do and not just what feels good; do not manipulate others to get your way.

➡ If you are interested in reading more on anger and aggression, explore the self-help and health sections of your library.

➡ Remember that not all anger is bad. Often it is necessary to change things. Nonviolent anger serves good purposes, but aggressive violence is rarely justified.

If You Have Tried All of This but It Has Not Helped . . .

If you have tried to reduce your anger and aggression but feel you need more help, talk to a counselor. You may need medication or someone to intervene on your behalf. Try not to feel helpless or hopeless.

Enhancing Your Ability to Cope

As you become older and more independent, you will make more decisions on your own behalf—hopefully healthy choices. Staying in good physical and mental health will put you in a better position to cope with life's stresses, including anger and aggression. Eating well, exercising, getting plenty of rest, and avoiding drugs and alcohol are just some sound choices you can make. Taking control of your physical, social, emotional, and spiritual health has many benefits.

Breathing

Breathing exercises can enhance your ability to cope throughout life. When you are feeling angry or are confronted with aggression, your mind can become agitated and your nervous system can be thrown off balance. Without realizing it, you might be holding your breath during the first moments of a stressful situation.

Decreasing oxygen to your cells affects your mind and body. Ordinarily, your breathing is automatic and requires no thinking on your part. From birth to death you breathe, steadily and continuously. With each inhalation and exhalation, carbon dioxide is burned and waste materials are eliminated from the blood. Breathing helps purify the bloodstream and supplies the blood with oxygen that body cells need. Your bones, nerves, muscles, skin, and glands all benefit.

Breathing energizes your body and has a positive effect on your emotional well-being. Breathing exercises enable you to cope more effectively with stress and increase your ability to concentrate. Stress can cause health problems like headaches or stomach disorders, and it can even lead to more serious ailments such as ulcers or high blood pressure. Prolonged stress can affect your immune system and lead to chronic disease. Focusing on your breathing is a simple and easy way of coping and relaxing.

By paying attention to your breathing, you can begin to feel more relaxed. Air should always be drawn in through your nose. The nose has special small hairs that filter dust, dirt, and bacteria. Breathing through the nose warms and moistens the air. As you breathe in, feel the cool air hitting the back of your throat. Breathing out, the breath feels warm. Just by focusing on your breathing, without doing anything to change it, promotes relaxation. As you develop a habit of breathing slowly and rhythmically, you will hone your ability to approach conflicts or challenges with loose, relaxed muscles and a calm mind.

Deep Breathing

Deep breathing relaxes your muscles while supplying additional oxygen to body cells. Give the following a try.

- Inhale deeply through your nose so it feels as if you are drawing breath toward your stomach. This will fill the lower lungs with oxygen.

- Continue to breathe in and expand the rib cage, filling the midlung area.

- Let your breath fill the upper portion of your lungs, lifting and expanding your chest.

- Pause for a second or two before exhaling, then exhale: first from the top portion, then middle, then push the air out of the lower lungs by contracting your abdominal muscles.

- Pause for a second and repeat the entire sequence a few more times.

Writing

Writing can help you emotionally and physically. Dr. James Pennebaker has researched how writing about stressful events can help heal both body and mind. His book, *Opening Up: The Healing Power of Confiding in Others* (Morrow, 1990), summarizes his research on how telling our stories and recording feelings benefits one's health. In one study, Pennebaker found that college students had better disease-fighting immunity after writing about stressful events.

It is believed that writing can help ease anger and give a person a sense of control and perspective. Chronicling not only an event but also how you feel about it can help diffuse your angry feelings. Left unprocessed, this anger could lead to aggressive behavior. You do not have to worry about spelling or grammar, just write, anytime.

Chad's parents were divorced. He lived with his mother and spent some weekends with his father. Chad loved to draw and paint flowers. This pleased his mother, but his father frowned at his canvases. Dad wanted his son to be an athlete.

Weekend visits were unpleasant. Chad could not draw or paint, and he could not pretend to be enthusiastic about the sports his dad watched on television and wanted to discuss. Chad would return to his mom's from these visits and feel sad and angry.

Chad could not discuss his feelings with his mother, so he started writing. In his room, he kept a notebook that was just for his writing. He would write in it as if he were talking to a friend. He would record things that happened and how they made him sad. He wrote for only about fifteen minutes, but even in that short time, he felt relieved and less angry.

Writing helped Chad to see that his parents are individuals with their own feelings, opinions, and personality quirks. Writing helped him cope with his parents, his weekend visits, and his father's disinterest in his art.

Through writing, you can develop a greater awareness of your feelings, which helps you manage and control them.

Do not let anger destroy you. Japanese literary theorist Zeami Motokiyo believes that writing cleanses the mind, enables the writer to achieve serenity, and purges tangled emotions. Writing can help you deal with your feelings of hopelessness, helplessness, and victimization.

As with writing, any method of coping can entail changing ways of thinking, addressing feelings, or taking action. Controlling your anger, reducing stress, problem solving, being assertive, practicing deep breathing exercises, and writing are only a few of the ways to begin handling your own aggressive impulses. If you are the victim of another's aggression, speak to someone who can intervene—a teacher, parent, or counselor. In either case, acknowledging the problem and finding sound ways to approach the situation will help.

Glossary

adolescence Time period between childhood and adult-hood when many physical, emotional, and intellectual changes occur.

aggression Verbal or physical action intended to harm another person or persons.

anger Hostile feelings caused by opposition or hurt.

assertiveness Ability to stand up for your rights without being aggressive.

bullying Form of aggression that may include such things as pushing, kicking, stealing, gossiping, embarrass-ing, spreading rumors, taunting, teasing, intimidating, or threatening.

chromosome Part of each cell in the body; contains deoxyribonucleic acid (DNA) and most or all of the genes of an individual.

conflict resolution Problem-solving strategy that seeks mutually acceptable solutions.

coping Thoughts, feelings, or actions taken to solve a problem or adapt to a situation.

depression Feelings of sadness that can be accompanied by aggression, moodiness, changes in sleep and eating habits, and suicidal thoughts.

electroencephalogram   Tracing of the brain's electrical activity.

hormones   Internally secreted compounds formed in certain body organs to promote proper body functions.

neurotransmitter   Chemical substance that transmits messages throughout the brain and body.

resiliency   Ability to recover from setbacks.

social learning theory   Belief that behaviors are learned by watching others.

sports rage   Aggressive behaviors committed by people at sporting events.

Where to Go for Help

In the United States

Al-Anon/Alateen
Family Group Headquarters
1600 Corporate Landing Parkway
Virginia Beach, VA 23454-5617
(888) 4AL-ANON (425-2666)
Web site: http://www.al-anon-alateen.org

American Academy of Child and Adolescent Psychiatry
3615 Wisconsin Avenue NW
Washington, DC 20016-3007
(202) 966-7300
Web site: http://www.aacap.org

American Council for Drug Education
164 West 74th Street

New York, NY 10023
(800) DRUG-HELP (378-4435)
Web site: http://www.acde.org

American Psychological Association
(800) 964-2000
Web site: http://www.helping.apa.org

Big Brothers Big Sisters of America
230 North 13th Street
Philadelphia, PA 19107
(215) 567-7000
Web site: http://www.bbbsa.org

Boys and Girls Clubs of America
1230 W. Peachtree Street NW
Atlanta, GA 30309
(404) 487-5700
Web site: http://www.bgca.org

Center to Prevent Handgun Violence
1225 Eye Street NW, Suite 1100
Washington, DC 20005
(202) 289-7319
Web site: http://www.cphv.org

Children and Adults with Attention Deficit/Hyperactivity
        Disorder (CHADD)
8181 Professional Place, Suite 201
Landover, MD 20785

(800) 233-4050
Web site: http://www.chadd.org

Children of the Night
14530 Sylvan Street
Van Nuys, CA 91411
(800) 551-1300
Web site: http://www.childrenofthenight.org

Covenant House
346 W. 17th Street
New York, NY 10011
(800) 999-9999
Web site: http://www.covenanthouse.org

Cult Awareness Network Hotline
(800) 556-3055
Web site: http://www.cultawarenessnetwork.org

Entertainment Software Rating Board
845 Third Avenue
New York, NY 10022
(800) 771-3772
Web site: http://www.esrb.org

Girls Incorporated
120 Wall Street, 3rd floor
New York, NY 10005-3902
(800) 374-4475
Web site: http://www.girlsinc.org

Head Injury Hotline
212 Pioneer Building
Seattle, WA 98104-2221
(206) 621-8558
Web site: http://www.headinjury.com

National Adolescent Suicide and Runaway Hotline
(800) 621-4000

National Campaign Against Youth Violence
Web site: http://www.noviolence.net

National Center for Conflict Resolution Education
424 South Second Street
Springfield, IL 62701
(800) 308-9419
Web site: http://www.nccre.org

National Child Abuse Hotline
(800) 422-4453

National Council on Alcoholism and Drug Dependence
20 Exchange Place, Suite 2902
New York, NY 10005
(800) NCA-CALL (622-2255)
Web site: http://www.ncadd.org

National Institute of Mental Health
6001 Executive Boulevard, Room 8184, MSC 9663
Bethesda, MD 20892-9663

(301) 443-4513
Web site: http://www.nimh.nih.gov

National Institute on Drug Abuse
6001 Executive Boulevard, Room 5213
Bethesda, MD 20892-9651
(301) 443-1124
Web site: http://www.nida.nih.gov

National Organization for Victim Assistance
1730 Park Road NW
Washington, DC 20010
(800) 879-6682
Web site: http://www.try-nova.org

National School Safety Center
141 Duesenberg Drive, Suite 11
Westlake Village, CA 91362
(805) 373-9977
Web site: http://www.nssc1.org

Office of Juvenile Justice and Delinquency Prevention
810 Seventh Street NW
Washington, DC 20531
(202) 307-5911
Web site: http://www.ojjdp.ncjrs.org

Rape, Abuse, and Incest National Network (RAINN)
635-B Pennsylvania Avenue SE
Washington, DC 20003
(800) 656-HOPE (4673)
Web site: http://www.rainn.org

Rape Crisis Center
(210) 349-7273
Web site: http://www.rapecrisis.com

Seeking Harmony in Neighborhoods Everyday (SHINE)
Web site: http://www.shine.excite.com

Student Pledge Against Gun Violence
112 Nevada Street
Northfield, MN 55057
Web site: http://www.pledge.org

Teen Letter Project
P.O. Box 936
Pacific Palisades, CA 90272
(301) 573-3655

Yellow Ribbon Suicide Prevention Program/Light for
        Life Foundation
P.O. Box 644
Westminster, CO 80036-0644
(303) 429-3530
Web site: http://www.yellowribbon.org

Young Men's Christian Association (YMCA)
Web site: http://www.ymca.net

In Canada

Al-Anon/Alateen
Web site: http://www.al-anon-alateen.org

Big Brothers and Big Sisters of Canada
3228 South Service Road, Suite 113E
Burlington, ON L7N 3H8
(800) 263-9133
Web site: http://www.bbsc.ca

Canadian Association of School Psychologists
162-2025 L'Avenue Corydon, Suite 252
Winnipeg, MB R3P 0N5
Web site: http://www.stemnet.nf.ca/casp

Canadian Psychological Association
151 Slater Street, Suite 205
Ottawa, ON K1P 5H3
(888) 472-0657
Web site: http://www.cpa.ca

Canadian Register of Health Service Providers
Web site: http://www.crhspp.ca

National Clearinghouse on Family Violence
Health Promotion and Programs Branch
1907 D1 Jeanne Mance Building, Tunney's Pasture
Ottawa, ON K1A 1B4
(800) 267-1291

National Youth in Care Network
202-327 Somerset Street West
Ottawa, ON K2P 0J8
(800) 790-7074
Web site: http://www.youthincare.ca

For Further Reading

Abner, Allison, and Linda Villarosa. *Finding Our Way: The Teen Girls' Survival Guide.* New York: HarperPerrenial, 1996.

Canfield, Jack, Mark Victor Hansen, and Kimberly Kirberger. *Chicken Soup for the Teenage Soul III.* Deerfield Beach, FL: Health Communications, 2000.

Carlson, Richard. *Don't Sweat the Small Stuff for Teens.* New York: Hyperion, 2000.

Covey, Sean. *The Seven Habits of Highly Effective Teens.* New York: Simon & Schuster, 1998.

Drill, Esther, Heather McDonald, and Rebecca Odes. *Deal with It! A Whole New Approach to Your Body, Brain, and Life as a Gurl.* New York: Pocket Books, 1999.

Eggert, Leona L. *Anger Management for Youth: Stemming Aggression and Violence.* Bloomington, IN: National Educational Service, 1994.

Freedom Writers, and Erin Gruwell. *The Freedom Writers Diary: How a Teacher and 150 Teens Used Writing to Change Themselves and the World Around Them.* New York: Doubleday, 1999.

Graham, Stedman. *Teens Can Make It Happen: Nine Steps to Success.* New York: Simon & Schuster, 2000.

Licata, Renora. *Everything You Need to Know About Anger.* Rev. ed. New York: The Rosen Publishing Group, Inc., 1999.

Mayall, Beth. *Get Over It: How to Survive Breakups, Back-Stabbing Friends, and Bad Haircuts.* New York: Scholastic Paperback, 2000.

Miller, Maryann. *Coping with Weapons and Violence in School and on Your Streets.* Rev. ed. New York: The Rosen Publishing Group, Inc., 1999.

Packer, Alex J. *How Rude! The Teenagers' Guide to Good Manners, Proper Behavior, and Not Grossing People Out.* Minneapolis, MN: Free Spirit Publishing, 1997.

Riera, Mike. *Surviving High School.* Berkeley, CA: Celestial Arts, 1997.

Shandler, Sara. *Ophelia Speaks: Adolescent Girls Write About Their Search for Self.* New York: HarperPerennial, 1999.

Tavris, Carol. *Anger: The Misunderstood Emotion.* Rev. ed. New York: Simon & Schuster, 1989.

Vizzini, Ned. *Teen Angst? Naaah: A Quasi-Autobiography.* Minneapolis, MN: Free Spirit Publishing, 2000.

Index

About the Author

Patricia Emanuele, R.N., has a master's degree in nursing and is a school nurse and health educator. She is the author of *Everything You Need to Know About Epilepsy* and lives in Basking Ridge, New Jersey.

Acknowledgments

I would like to acknowledge the following people for assisting me in the creation of this book: my dear friend and former colleague Eileen Valinoti, R.N., for her inspiring nature and talented editing; Rekha Gandhi, MLS, and the staff of New Jersey's Morristown Memorial Hospital Library for their research assistance; Daniela DiCarlo, M.A., school psychologist, for her valued professional feedback; and my friends and family for their support. I would especially like to thank my daughter, Vanessa, and my sister, Janet Stutski, for their constant love and encouragement in making this book possible.